STARK LIBRARY NOV

ANIMALS WITH SUPERPOWERS!

REGENERATE!

WRITTEN BY **EMILIE DUFRESNE**
DESIGNED BY **AMY LI**

Published in 2022 by
KidHaven Publishing,
an Imprint of Greenhaven Publishing, LLC
353 3rd Avenue
Suite 255
New York, NY 10010

© 2022 Booklife Publishing
This edition is published by arrangement with Booklife Publishing

All rights reserved. No part of this book may be reproduced in any form without permission in writing from the publisher, except by a reviewer.

Find us on

Cataloging-in-Publication Data

Names: Dufresne, Emilie.
Title: Regenerate! / Emilie Dufresne.
Description: New York : KidHaven Publishing, 2022. | Series: Animals with superpowers! | Includes glossary and index.
Identifiers: ISBN 9781534534971 (pbk.) | ISBN 9781534534995 (library bound) | ISBN 9781534534988 (6 pack) | ISBN 9781534535008 (ebook)
Subjects: LCSH: Animal behavior--Juvenile literature. | Adaptation (Biology)--Juvenile literature. | Animal defenses--Juvenile literature.
Classification: LCC QL751.5 D847 2022 | DDC 591.5--dc23
Printed in the United States of America

CPSIA compliance information: Batch #CS22KH: For further information contact Greenhaven Publishing LLC, New York, New York at 1-844-317-7404.

Please visit our website, www.greenhavenpublishing.com. For a free color catalog of all our high-quality books, call toll free 1-844-317-7404 or fax 1-844-317-7405.

PHOTO CREDITS All images courtesy of Shutterstock. With thanks to Getty Images, Thinkstock Photo and iStockphoto.

Cover – Azamatovic, Lazerko A, UltraViolet, Zorana Matijasevic, Tiny Doz. Vector Animals – natchapohn, Andrew Rybalko (Professor Ax), Guz Anna (starfish, spider), StockSmartStart (deer, moose), Rvector (lizard), mckenna71 (shark). Master images – TinyDoz (header font), Azamatovic, Natalisa (main and panel backgrounds), Zorana Matijasevic, UltraViolet (Comic bubbles, assets and annotations), Nata Alhontess (Speech bubbles and boxes), Lazerko A (page number cloud). 1 – Lazerko A, 2-3 – Nata Alhontess, 4-5 – james weston, 6-7 – elenabsl, Kastoluza, WhiteDragon, enjoy your life, Good_Stock, 8-9 – Anna Frajitova, dovla982, Terry Virbickis, popovartem.com, 10-11 – pikepicture, Baksiabat, Nadzin, nicolasvoisin44, 12-13 – iSKYDANCER, KittyVector, Nutkins J, 14-15 – Alexey Pushkin, StockSmartStart, Federico.Crovetto, Eric Isslee, 16-17 – jopelka, pikepicture, Baksiabat, 18-19 – sciencepics, Sarawutt Padungkwan, 20-21 – DRogatnevm WhiteDragon, Kazakov Maksim, Nadzin, 22-23 – mhatzapa, james weston

CONTENTS

PAGE 4	Superheroes of the Future
PAGE 6	Regeneration
PAGE 8	Deer
PAGE 10	Sharks
PAGE 12	Spiders
PAGE 14	Lizards
PAGE 16	Starfish
PAGE 18	Flatworms
PAGE 20	Axolotls
PAGE 22	The Next Generation
PAGE 24	Glossary and Index

Words that look like *this* can be found in the glossary on page 24.

SUPERHEROES OF THE FUTURE

The world is constantly under threat. Whether it's from crime, alien invasions, or humans destroying the planet, one thing is known for certain. Something has got to change...

SHARKS

Sharks are apex predators in the oceans. They have a vicious bite that can rip out their teeth. But you will never see a toothless shark...

Let's use the hammerhead shark as an example.

10

Hammerhead sharks have rows of tiny, sharp teeth in their mouths. A hammerhead shark can lose and regrow around **30,000** teeth in its lifetime.

FACT FILE

NAME: Hammerhead shark

LIVES: **Tropical** and **coastal** waters around the world

SIZE: From 36 inches (90 cm) to over 20 feet (6.1 m) long

SUPERPOWER: Rows and rows of teeth that can be replaced

SPIDERS

Spiders can choose to lose legs to help them get away from **predators**. This is called autotomy. Some spiders, like the huntsman spider, can grow these legs back.

But how do they do this?

I don't want to know.

Before a spider **molts**, any lost legs are regrown inside its **exoskeleton**.

BZZZZ!

I may only have seven legs, but i'm still going to eat you!

NAME:	Huntsman spider
LIVES:	Warm, **temperate** areas: Australia, Africa, Asia, and the Americas
SIZE:	A leg **span** of up to 11.8 inches (30 cm)
SUPERPOWER:	Can grow back lost limbs

13

In around 100 days, her tail will have grown back

Day 1

Day 100

NAME: Common wall lizard
LIVES: Dry, rocky areas of Europe and North America
SIZE: Up to 7.9 inches (20 cm) long, including tail
SUPERPOWER: Can grow back tail

AXOLOTLS

We axolotls have some of the best regeneration powers out there. We can regenerate bones, tissue, and even our brains and spines.

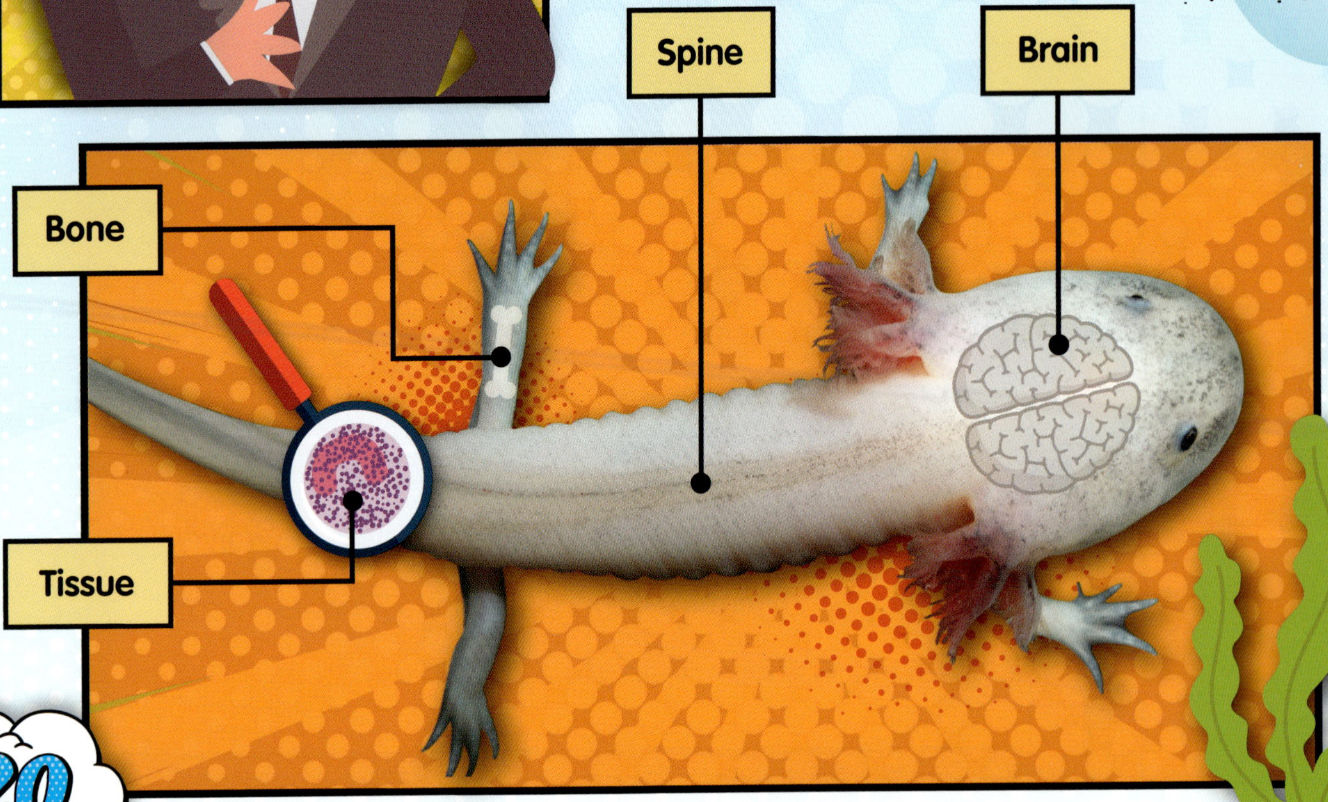

Spine

Brain

Bone

Tissue

Every regeneration is nearly perfect, and hardly ever leaves behind any scar tissue.

FACT FILE

NAME: Axolotl (say: ax-oh-lot-ul) or water dog

LIVES: Lakes and canals in Mexico

SIZE: Up to 17.7 inches (45 cm) long

SUPERPOWER: Perfect regeneration, mostly without any scar tissue

GLOSSARY

apex predators — animals that are at the top of the food chain and are not prey for another animal
coastal — describing the area where the land and the ocean meet
exoskeleton — a hard structure on the outside of a creature
generation — a group of people that have a similar age or are involved in a particular activity
limbs — arms and legs, as well as the wings of birds
molts — sheds a layer of skin, hair, feathers, or bone and grows a new covering
predators — animals that eat other animals for food
scar tissue — a thick layer of tissue that is formed when healing a wound and is different from the original tissue
span — the distance stretched between two points
temperate — describing a region or climate that is characterized by mild temperatures
tissue — groups of cells that are similar to each other and do the same job
tropical — a hot and humid region

INDEX

antlers	8–9	Mexico	21
Australia	13	oceans	7, 10, 17
autotomy	12, 14	predators	10, 12, 14
copies	6, 19	regrow	6, 9, 11, 13, 17
fur	9	scar tissue	21
legs	12–13	tails	14–15
limbs	6, 13	teeth	10–11

24